Marjorie Main

Rural Documentary Poetry

John Sherman

MESA VERDE PRESS

INDIANAPOLIS

Please direct inquiries to:
Mesa Verde Press
4175 Central Avenue
Indianapolis, IN 46205
shermco@earthlink.net

First Edition

Published in the United States of America.

Designed by Jinny Bastianelli,
The Electronic Studio, Indianapolis

Library of Congress Card Number: 99-091362

ISBN 0-9607220-1-7

Acknowledgments

The original manuscript of *Marjorie Main* earned John Sherman a Finalist position in the 1981 Walt Whitman Award competition sponsored by the Academy of American Poets. This book is a somewhat expanded version of that manuscript.

The following poems first appeared in these publications:

"The Land" in *San Marcos Press Broadsheet*

"I Never Ate Chicken Livers" in *Berkeley Review*

"World of Women" in *Santa Fe Poetry*

"Reminiscences 1958-1960: To My Former English Teacher Who Is Retiring" in *NEBO*

"Blackberry Winter" in *Arts Indiana*

"Tile" in *Indiana Writes*

"Drinking Cup" in *Flying Island*

"Marjorie Main" and "Spoon" were published in my poetry book, *It Give You Something To Think About*.

"Marjorie Main" was awarded first-place honors in the Writers' Center of Indianapolis "Poetry in the Gallery" competition in 1999.

Books by John Sherman

It Give You Something To Think About (1977)

America Is A Negro Child: Race Poems (Mesa Verde Press, 1981)

Santa Fe: A Pictorial History (Donning, 1983, 1996)

Taos: A Pictorial History (Gannon, 1990)

Introduction

These poems, for the most part, reflect some of my experiences while growing up on my parents' farm in Jay County, Indiana, from the mid-1940s to the early 1960s. They are placed in the book in chronological order. The first poem, "The Land," was written by hand in a spiral notebook as I lay on my dormitory bed at Indiana University, waiting for a ride home for Thanksgiving in 1963, one day after I had returned from President John F. Kennedy's funeral in Washington, D.C. The last one, "Cottonwood," was written on a computer in Indianapolis during the summer of 1998, the year my sisters and I helped my parents sort out the possessions of several generations as they prepared to sell their farm and move to a retirement community. (Not having fully come to terms with the fact that my boyhood home — and my father's boyhood home — has been sold, I have designated this a poem "in progress," as I have probably not yet finished writing about that topic.) In the intervening 35 years, poems were written wherever I was living at the time – Nigeria, Malawi, Ghana, Zaire, Washington, D.C., or Santa Fe – or on airplanes over mountains or oceans, as I sat and thought about my childhood. One, "April Afternoon," seized me when I stepped off a bus coming home from work in Washington, D.C.

I was encouraged to publish these poems as a collection because they have been well received whenever I have read them. I was often told that I had captured the universality of experience, even though the persons telling me this had often grown up in vastly different circumstances – raised in big-city apartments or suburban homes, reared in much wealthier circumstances, members of ethnic groups not a part of my childhood, or members of older or younger generations. Yet, I was told, this was *their* grandmother I had written about, *their* fears or joys, albeit experienced in Manhattan or Denver.

I also wanted to publish these poems because they describe a way of life that has all but disappeared: when radio reigned, party-line telephones were cranked to get "Central," one's father could, as mine did, sleep in the very room in which he had been born, and almost everything (including ketchup) was homemade.

When I wrote these poems, I took myself back there, and every time I read them, I return. I invite you to read them and go there as well.

John Sherman
Indianapolis
October 1999

Dedication

To my maternal grandparents, Mary Etta and John Scholer, who live on in my rich memories, and to my uncle, Dale Scholer, whose generosity helped make this book possible.

Poems

The Land 1

This Is I 2

County Fair: A Prose Poem 4

I Knew A Jew 7

A Philco Ad 9

I Never Ate Chicken Livers As A Group 13

Anthology 16

World of Women 21

Reminiscences 1958-60:

To My Former English Teacher Who Is Retiring 24

July 29

Idea 31

April Afternoon 35

Marjorie Main 38

Blackberry Winter 41

Wes and Nory 43

Twine 47

Ketchup 49

Tile 51

Spoon 53

Memories 55

Boots 58

Bemberg or Nylon 63

Crusts 66

I Want To Write Poems 69

Drinking Cup 72

The Prettiest 73

Crayons 74

Back Home 75

Tell Them This When I Die 76

Cottonwood 77

THE LAND

I shall never forget the land
the open spaces to roam at will
seeing squirrels rabbits and neighbor dogs
on forbidden jaunts through
leaves brush and dying streams

no polluted air
save the acrid smell of newly fertilized fields
no noises of next door neighbors
save the putt putt cough putt
of an early morning tractor

the privilege of sitting on a wet warm stream bank
and contemplating why
seeing the water run on and on and on
guessing its start and finish

from the crust of the earth stand proud green cornstalks
waiting to tassle
give up their fruit
and fall in golden brown skeletons to their mother

the trees are big
grotesque
old friends
standing
waiting to be
climbed
shot at
swung from
dogpissed on
chopped down
and firewooded

THIS IS I

I am akin to flower sellers
and smile wrinkled peasants

my poetry springs from such
because I am such

words I write come from fields

I am akin to beauty
and to beastliness
the dew on the grass is as much me
as the bleating of new wethers

put me in cities
and I am smelling hay
and remembering birthing lambs
and ever so gently uncrating chicks

but don't call me farmer
without meaning the meaning
I want
for farmer yelled
is nigger yelled
to those ghetto pigmented
and I bristle when people are surprised
at origins apparently disguised
as if farmers were but bumpkins
staring at bigger than hometown buildings

but I have known too much
of the grapes of wrath
worried weather watching hand wringing
over single frail animal deaths
kind of rural people

too much of cholesterol picnics
and well helping sick
and late night mortgage eyes
wondering where the next farm was coming from

to excuse jeers of sidewalk bred
who never saw the beauty
of a lamb's first step
or wheat upon wheat
dancing in the wind

who never saw the tragedy of tears
shed on egg checks
when prices dropped
who never saw women trapped in houses
that acres couldn't release
with flocks of children
and herds of dishes

or young men nosed in books
fighting against suffocations
not wishing to share

all of it
good and sad
has made me:

this is I

COUNTY FAIR

a prose poem

---

hawkers hawking japanese junk

carnies they were called by us locals

kewpie dolls whose heads fell off
once safely away from the midway
turn on toys that lost their power
when demonstrations attempted later

once I spent phenomenally
two dollars I think it was
on a girl trying to win a teddy bear
threw the three for a quarter balls
and threw and threw
the next night
an athlete won her two teddy bears and
a fake flower for her long tresses
I was never allowed to caress again

threw up each time I rode the octopus
every year the same
tirades from mother
who didn't accept my determination
nor my soiled clothes

it's all in your head
she said
well I knew it was no more
in my stomach
yet patience
on top of grim I told you sos
since my condition was inherited

even for a farm boy the massive sows were marvels
couldn't believe the length of those heaving panting bodies
seeming hundreds of teats sewn up and down

all over the grounds
fresh tar caramel corn hogs and vomit
came whiffing up one's nostrils

certain smells even now
caught suddenly bring flashes
to mind of walking endlessly
around the fair staring when young
at boy girl held hands and
returning stares when older

one's diet consisted of everything but balance
candy cane that disappeared and left sugar crusts on lips
candy apples that fought with one's teeth
warning them of the sour greenness to come
caramel corn to munch and spill on paths already strewn
snow cones that started out round and cold
and ended as pools of red or green in
rotting cup bottoms

4-H exhibits will always hold special meaning
having done them myself
staying up late the night before due
painting and gluing and printing
and reaping yearly admonitions
for not having done things when time was there
but playing tag in twilight
or reading books on blankets under
trees with summer dead leaves hitting
leaves was my choice

my night before act gave me my
project to present to the eyebrow
raised judges who noted my wetness and
graded accordingly

my records were good
my projects were not

one goes back now as observer and catches the smells
and sees oneself on kiddie rides
or walking with girls
or staring at sows
or displaying animals

one year the judge pushed on the spine
of my loosely held sheep and it bolted
amid giggles from others
at that moment I hated sheep
and judges equally

and for too brief moments
one not only remembers but is
and the sweetness and sorrow
of all those fairs
return
but then the present scene focuses
and instead of self
one sees one's own children
giggling and smelling and eating

and throwing up

I KNEW A JEW

I knew a jew
in my hometown
who was utterly destroyed
by not being able to hide
his name
his father

by having utter strangers
gazing and guessing
and outright asking

he was
boxed
hemmed
squeezed
into his jewishness
kicking and screaming
and the town auschwitzed his mind
and made him a partial being
and a zero jew

to them he was a yid
and never could the twain meet
  (he could date their daughters
   but not without enduring first
   those questions in those parlors
   while he waited on that last
   brushing of golden hair
   and then not for too many dates
   in a row)

and all his appearances
at sunday school
could but point out the differences and
his shylock father
rubbing his stereotyped hands
at the front door of his surnamed store

was but a neon sign
in the night
planted like a burning star of david
across the lawn of his mind

I knew a jew
and it frightened me
to see this ethnic thing
loom so important
in the tiny minds of those
who prayed and preyed
and I fled a jew myself
or so it seemed

A PHILCO AD

in a magazine the other day
I saw a philco ad:
buy a copy of our 1930s radio
it said
and
the knobs
the dark wood
the grille
the immensity
of what it is now
transistorized computerized and pocketed
drew me back and threw me back
to days of running up the long gravel lane
from the dust covered inside and out
yellow bus
forty five minutes after leaving our
two classes to a room schoolhouse

I played spaceman in the back seat
with fellow martians
where bolts and screws
became instrument indicators
and bounces from potholes
were thrusts of the mighty rocket engines

(and I remember a boy
whose name I have now forgotten
who lived across the road from the arnolds
in a tarpaper shack
who was moving away in the middle of the year
as the tarpaper kids tended to do
and I was crying on the bus
on the last day of our existence
and he pulled my head up by my front hair
and saw my tears and
he stared hard

bit his lip
and produced his own
and I watched him walk to his front door
only yards from the road
and waved him out of my life
and rested my chin on my arms
folded over the rocket panel
and idly drew circles around a crayoned mark
made stealthily by someone defying
the sharpeyed driver
and waited for the bus
to drop me off
in front of our lane
that was just right in spring and fall
but miles long in winter snows)

and running up the lane
was a nightly race with the dog
and we always tied
gracefully barkingly laughingly
at the kitchen door
through which I ran dropping my coat and
retrieving it at my mother's command
before coming to a reverent halt in front of
that magic box to catch
the 4:30 programs and beyond

trivia games of late send me into frenzies
as I am recalled
to tonto
to the masked man
to hi ho silver
(who was that masked man the voices asked
and I shouted in glee the lone ranger
and then eveready batteries saved nine lives
people caught in floods hurricanes darkened buildings
always found two evereadys in
their glove compartments handbags desk drawers
and I for a long time planned

to carry two with me
when I grew up in case
I got stranded somewhere
and had to rescue that fabled fair damsel
who would no doubt ditch me
as being too weird
for having carried two batteries
around in my pants pocket
my claiming I was waiting
for just such a moment
or more likely I would have the batteries
but the flashlight would be safe in the trunk
of my black '98
sinking slowly in the quicksand)

sky king
taking off in his airplane
saving penny from all those disasters
and quaker puffed wheat
sank soggily into my consciousness
and jingles were hummed or ignored
as I trimmed my toenails
forbiddenly on the carpet
or looked at colliers
and waited for penny to be saved
as I knew she would
yet I wanted to make sure
before I ran outside to tear around the house
with pooch the dog in hot mock pursuit
running past the window from where my mother shouted
at me to feed the chickens or whatever
we were raising that week

at night deep voice dave garroway for dial soap
summer brought stella dallas pushing organ music
and daily trauma
sunday the fbi and the shadow
and I listened to them with an eye on the door
and sighed with relief that it wasn't dark

though if parents were napping
it was felt wise to have a fellow listener

I saw that philco ad
and I remembered our big as hell
wooden radio with the zillion knobs
and the woven webbed front
through which the glimmer of the tubes
and the magic of the world crept
but the desire for the new philco look alike
never stirred

for how could one recapture sky king 1952

and today mary noble backstage wife
would have hysterectomies
and no one would understand
that a gossipy neighbor but
intimating things over air waves
could send such delicious thoughts
into housewives' minds
and allow fingers to caress too carefully
the dough being kneaded in kitchens
heavy with smells of fruits canning
and children waiting to go outside to play

I NEVER ATE CHICKEN LIVERS
AS A GROUP

I never ate chicken livers as a group
but only one by one
with chicken gizzards and chicken wings
and chicken legs and chicken thighs
and dry white meat breasts
that pulled off the bone in one large piece
and went down with
lots of water
and lots of chewing

I never ate chicken livers as livers
but as part of the whole damned hen
and the thought of buying
only that anatomical portion
would have retched me
one who didn't care that much for livers anyway
and who tried to hide them sometimes
under the plate or discreetly between
two finished wings and three legs
stacked in front of me
as if
deformed as it were
the chicken had crawled up there
and died

I never ate mushrooms
(we were always afraid of toadstools
 those funny scary things we wouldn't even touch
 that we found at the foot of tall dark trees
 back in our woods)

I never ate mushrooms
but solid fruit pies after
the mashed potatoes
gravy

fried chicken
two vegetables
and hot rolls
buttered
to fill up the crevices between
my too many belt loops

mushrooms were something marveled at
in magazine ads and pondered about
when the conversation ran down on a tuesday night
in winter when nothing interesting was on the radio
and it was too early for decent people to go to bed

heads were shaken and one would wonder aloud
who and where and for what reason on earth
people would eat such things
and someone would offer to bring in
the rest of the pie
and a couchful and two chairsful of hands would
go up volunteering to assist in the finishing off
of the pieces sitting in the fridge
and we would devour the creation of the afternoon
and dig with our forks
at the now rubbery hard juices
stuck to the glass pie plate
trying to force free the little bit that was left
and the bits of crust stuck to the edge of the plate
would disappear into mouths now silent

and the time would pass
and another radio program would come on which we liked
and we would be transported into worlds
out of our reach where people ate mushrooms
and chicken livers all in a heap
and didn't know the simple pleasure of leftover
almost cold apple pie
on a winter night a tuesday perhaps
somewhere in a flowery rugged living room

with tiny crumbs of crust
sprinkled ever so lightly on the chairs
to be brushed off with abrupt hands
the next morning and sped to the trash can
peeling its exterior away
in the corner of the kitchen
where more pies lay in the oven gurgling
in their own juices
and noses perked up and eyes lighted
as the flavor was determined
and supper looked forward to

ANTHOLOGY

don't scott foresman me
with footnotes and guesstimates
about what I said lines and years ago
don't holt reinhart my words
and force kids to mumble them
when they want to be outside
playing ball
or balling

(how I dreaded reading poetry
 from those heavy books
 that encompassed centuries of literature
 force fed to those of us
 who might have learned
 had we not been so frantically taught
 who might have enjoyed the flow
 and the rhyme had we not been
 made to study the fine print
 and the editor's scribbling
 set down in italic pica)

I don't want my poetry to be included
in those haughty books
I don't want years
and acres of scholars
to avoid me
I don't want to be the subject
of a command to read
page such and such for monday
met with groans from students
more interested in living
their own poems over the weekend

I want to be discovered
in a book of my own pulled from the shelf
in a house or a library or a shop
I want to be awed at

and laughed over
and puzzled about
and bought or borrowed
or even stolen
(provided the royalties have
 already been paid)

but spare me the assignments on
vapid white paper of what I was
saying in this poem or that
spare me the interpretations
of those high school english
teachers who think of poetry
as possessed by pale women
writing with quill pen
so many inventions ago
or men who are suspected of
lacking the right amount
of starch in that joint
that connects their arm
and their hand that sets
it all down

spare me those teachers who don't know
what I am saying but who insist on not
only deciding anyway but not allowing
other opinions to interfere

and don't number my lines
or footnote my words
or biographicize me
until I and my poems are
dried shriveled and dead

rather I would not publish at all
than be condemned to condemn a
student to the torture of having
to read a medium he has been
taught to mistrust

a poet of whom he has never heard
a poem of which he has no desire
to dissect chew up and choke on

my poems are not meant for such
let them be
let them be just as they are
let them breathe outside the confines
of columns entitled questions to answer
and notes on this poem
boxed in by those english majors
who cannot write worth a damn themselves
because they cannot get their noses
out of the how not to do it books
that give them their grammatical hard ons

unhand me
unhand my poems
I am free
and so are they
and let's keep it that way

are you reading me now
for the first time
standing in a library corner
perhaps somewhere in iowa
holding your legs together
because you've got to pee
but too curious about me
to put me down and go away
even for the length of one urination

or was this on a sale counter
in a posh shop east of the mississippi
mixed in with animal books
and art books
that one finds
at such places at such times
am I the token poetry volume

put here to make the store seem intellectual
yet the only one so the public to which
it so carefully caters won't
think it too deep and go away

or perhaps
perhaps you are sitting on a log
letting the warm mid morning breeze
blow through your hair
recovering from winter
and restless with the damp spring
beginning to feel the beginnings of poetry
in yourself and so you have fled a school
as I did once in a teenage spring
and you are reading me instead
of notebooks and notices
of proms and play rehearsals

once I left school and read keats
sitting on a log on one of those spring
days that make you sweat and wish
you were other places and older
and I read him aloud turning around
occasionally to make sure no neighbor
sneaking into the woods for rabbits
or squirrels would hear me and
think of me worse than he already did

for that morning I was calm
my dog my audience
sitting reverently
and only once in a while making a noise
when he needed to sneeze or comment
on the appropriateness of such
a romantic choice
for that morning I was calm
and I read him aloud
lustily and then softly

and something stirred in me
that I am only now releasing

perhaps
perhaps then
you are sitting on a log

know that I am not pleased
for pleased is much too mild
a word for what I feel
I am flabbergasted
I am of that mood that makes me
shove my hand into my mouth
and gasp and blink back tiny tears
and take a quick breath then another
and feel the back of my neck
my own damp hair
and wish I were there to hear
you read me aloud
to the birds and the moss
and to all that is rural and me

WORLD OF WOMEN

I am doomed to a world of women
one wife
one daughter
three sisters and
a mother

no brothers shared the womb
and no sons shared the seed
I was the last of us four
and my father said he did not look
at my face for a week
to which my mother always replied
with her oh john
her hand brought up to catch a laugh
but her hand there nevertheless
necessary to show that
while her god permits a little fun
he prefers it doesn't run amuck

I was the last of us four
and did not suffer handmedowns
or share boyfriends
or giggly gossip
in the north room upstairs
I ran the creek with my dog
glad I wasn't a girl
to sit in the north room
though I did wish dogs could talk back
with something other than their ears
and tails and eternal sardonic smiles

right now it's just
me
my wife
and daughter

and the latter is the boss of the ranch
telling us when to get up
when to sleep
when to go to the kitchen
(not that a son would be any different)
 I used to run our house I'm sure
crowing in hoosier what I wanted
from my iron day bed off the kitchen
where we pumped water
made soap
canned the south forty
or so it seemed

and baked enough bread
so no miracles would be necessary
if jesus came to call
(so long as he brought his own fish)
where we acted out our self sufficient lives
a generation later than the rest of the country
and did not know
we had been passed by
until we at last turned to plastic
and found the others returning to wood

I am doomed to a world of women
not complaining mind you
just relating
that part of my history
so that when you see the agency deliver a boy
and see my mighty grin
you'll understand that my son will be my brother
in a manner of being a companion against
hair curlers and gossip in all those
north rooms up all those stairs
past and present
and if you want us you'll do well
to go downstairs and outside
on the front where we'll be sitting

talking men talk about such things
as poetry and sunsets
and running collies to the creek

REMINISCENCES 1958 - 1960:

To My Former English Teacher Who Is Retiring

I.

each day
fifth period
in one of those tiny
hot rooms upstairs
we were enthralled
by a white haired
country rough
city smooth
teacher
with gentle but snappy eyes
that didn't miss
what wasn't to be missed
a big woman with a
church choir voice
loud and liquid rich
breaking down now and again
into laughter that was infectious

yet sometimes in other classes
down the hall
we could hear
her exercising it against
those who did something
they thought she hadn't seen

II.

for two years she dragged me
kicking and screaming
through the english language
rubbing my nose in it
until I came up smelling verbs

III.

she even made silas marner interesting
a fitting epitaph for any teacher
the stone would say that
and no more would need be said

IV.

I remember a boy who sat in the back of the room
who looked like a pig
we had boys who were discards
who survived until they were sixteen
and maybe by then in the ninth grade
who couldn't answer the simplest of questions
who smelled
who were treated by her
as if they were human beings

V.

I never felt closer to her
than that first time I went to teach
I yelled and sweated and loved
and wrote her a letter that began:
dear fellow teacher
and was ever so proud to begin it that way

it made me even more determined
to go see her
whenever I went back to the town
I knew what it meant
one could talk of anything
you could even be nervous
and stay only a short time
but you had to stop
and say without saying it:
thank you for being where you were
when you were

I am here now
whatever I am
a part of you

VI.

I would sweat through my lesson plans
asking myself what she would have done
how I could be like her
some days I succeeded with a fervor
I would come home shaking
unable to sit down
smoke one cigarette after another
read my mail
write fast furious letters to friends
exclaiming my love for the profession
that I run to and from
here and there

other days it would drag
I would be upset
and sit quietly in the corner
hunched over a book
to try to forget
that I was not she today
but merely me and that was not enough

VII.

have you ever gone back to a school
that you loved and cared about
more than anything else
at that moment in your life
to find it dead

I leaned against a pillar
with a piece of grass in my teeth
and looked at memories go running by:

students crowding at the library door
or devouring animal farm
or laughing with me
in the early evening
when the shadows of those pillars
lay down and stretched all the way
to the dining hall

I wondered how many she had seen
go to vietnam and never return
I wondered how many she had seen
go up in smoke in a dual vehicle crash
that kicked bodies and minds out of the machines
to float one glorious last time through the air
I wondered how we were able to stand
seeing all those other people go
and I felt it not fair
it seemed all so obscene
that they should go first

and I knew then the sorrows of being a teacher
of seeing all those dreams of all those students
end with a doctor's nod that someone
indeed was pregnant or dead

VIII.

there was a girl in our freshman english class
who left us that spring to have a child
it scared all but two or three more
before we commenced to cap and gown
ourselves into life

when we saw this girl later
her almond eyes
sad enough in the best of times
bore into us and made us
turn away
feel guilty

that it were not us
so that she might have been spared

I thought of her the day last fall
when my first child was born
fourteen years after her first
and all I had been
freed to do

for a moment
I resented myself
I resented my child
until the overwhelmingness of my event
turned thoughts to a new immediate family

IX.

when teachers leave their desks
the final time
I wonder if they don't stop
at the door
their arms laden with gifts from
their last students
and look hard into the room
to see the faces of those
of us who came before
some of us dead
some struggling with children born too soon
some sitting at a typewriter
making a poem about an english teacher
classrooms and classrooms ago

JULY

I have always been a little afraid
of july I suppose
because of the electrical storms
I endured as a child
sitting with siblings in the kitchen
puppy huddled around mother
shivering when the
lightning flashed and cracked
across the sky
counting the seconds between flashes and pops
to determine how close they were
and finding ourselves outcounted sometimes
as the false daylight would hit our front porch
and knock that electrical thing off the wall
time and time again

when dad was there
we didn't huddle but only spoke
more softly and carried lamps and flashlights
around the farmhouse giving halloween scenery
to non october nights

but with him gone it was necessary
to group ourselves and shake
praying for the storm to go away
and come again when we were not there
and it was not until I as an adult
faced the storms that I realized
that my mother was as frightened
as we all were
and must have drawn comfort
from four warm bodies near her
our need of her strength giving her hers

heat lightning was bad enough
flashing spastically in the western sky

outlined against the trees on the hill
we could see through the small bathroom window
but the real crackerjack electrical storms
with the brilliant smashing light that let us
see the barn in unreal detail and the
loud horrible noise of the thunder
coming at us again and again and again
was something that still draws me
away from windows and
makes me sit in walled rooms
in the middle on a dry wooden chair
with rubber leg tips as I count the seconds
knowing not how close it was
but only that once again I wasn't hit

I live in the tropics now
we have rain by the ton
and other things to scare us
and thunder is a surprise
said in sentences like:
was that thunder or an airplane
and it is with the greatest
of relief that I face july
sitting proudly defiantly near windows
with my feet wet touching metal
my tongue aimed at the sky in
a bronx cheer that I am not
condemned to an indiana farmhouse
to wait out the month
until sultry languid august
takes over too lazy
I suppose to
conjure up the displays in the sky
that july had so rudely given us once again

IDEA

she looked like an idea whose time had come
and gone
leaning in the doorway
in a posture that could only mean despair
on a farm in a county that was nowhere

fuller brushman I said
got some new brushes

opening my case I was sure this was a lost cause
but what the hell I was an hour ahead
of what I thought I would be
so why not chat and pass on gossip
and maybe get some too

don't need none she said
forcing the words out
as if it were a magnificent effort
to operate one's vocal cords
yet she stared mighty hard
at the same time
at the green and red handled brushes
I was now holding up in front of her
needed ironing dress

good for scrubbing floors I said
pointing one at her own
then admonishing myself for letting it look
as if I thought she didn't know what I meant
good for scrubbing floors
and waited for the next response
which came too fast not to have been thought out
ahead of time:

how much

not an unusual question of course

they asked it all the time
funny how the women wouldn't even touch the brush
before wanting to know how much it cost
no use wasting the effort of feeling the stiff bristles
or the plastic curved handle
if there wasn't enough money under the mattress

not much I said
how much is not much
one ninety five I lied
and even two dollars less than real
caused her face to sag
at one more defeat one more morning
one ninety five
slowly said
sounded a fortune

only got sixty five cents
she said
and brushed back her hair
revealing a speckled sunburned forehead
not seen before

well that won't hardly do now will it
said yours truly the great conversationalist
sixty five cents
I don't have anything for that amount
I said
pretending to try to find
something in the satchel
already deciding to give her a free sample
of something I had there for paying customers
and call it a trade

nothing at all
she mocked me without
meaning to mock
but merely repeated my empty phrase
about an empty bag

I need that brush she said
tossing back her hair
a fine head of hair it was
long and black and silky
I noticed next
her toe curling against the floor
drawn up then to scratch some place
on the other leg
scratching slowly

my eyes crept
up her leg past her pelvis
to her reasonable chest
to her eyes
dark too
olive sort of

she ran her tongue against her upper teeth
and said too calmly:
take it out in trade

(at times like that I am accustomed
to asking what someone said
as I am never sure that what was said
was truly said and I want to be sure
before I react too extremely
to something not heard well)

take it out in trade
she said more loudly
waiting for my response

for the brush she added
afraid I guess that I would
make her and the trade one sided

for one brush
I said to the woman now looking
like an idea whose time had come

I snickered and bit my lip
then scratched my ear
suddenly unable to look at her again
until she said something
to break the silence

yeah she said
yeah I said in return

well she said I ain't got all day
sort of bette davis like
tapping one foot on the boards

okay I said walking up the steps
and onto the creaking porch
being careful to bring my bag with me
so I wouldn't leave it out in the yard
for who knows what

so for a three ninety five brush
I took a woman to bed
in a smallish run down house
in the middle of nowhere

and just before I walked out the door
my bag in my hand
I saw all the other brushes
lined on the sill hot and black in the sun
and laughed to myself
reached in my bag
threw a handful of free samples
on the horsehair chair
waved goodbye
banged the screen door
and walked away

a full fledged fuller brush salesman

APRIL AFTERNOON

there is a tenseness in this too warm april afternoon
and that with the smell of the threat of rain
remembers me to those grade school noons
when I sat praying hard that it would pour
so that I would not have to go onto the diamond
and expose and display my awkward attempts
to try to catch or pitch a ball

I served in right field
where I could do the least harm
where the balls rarely came
so I could stand
and mentally write my next book report
and be alone for moments
until that horrible sight
of a left handed batter
would come into my view
and the screams of my teammates
would warn me to be ready
and the other team would laugh
knowing that I was the dunce
of their opponents

and for one moment both sides were joined
in making fun of a fat kid
with glasses and a glove
hitching up his belt
trying to disappear into the sparse grass
knowing he would never in his life
catch the ball about to come his way

and he was right

I would invoke my god
to bring rain
to stop the game
even before it began

but I cannot remember ever
being answered
with anything but
clouds passing over
on their way
to someone else's outfield

(and I can never go by a playground in motion
 without thinking hard of those children out there
 who are standing waiting their turns
 to strike out)

at lunch eaten at our desks
the talk would be of the game
and my stomach would tighten
and I would stare at the glove
at my foot
not knowing whether to hate it
or feel it was a companion
to be with me in the field

it was too small
just one more thing to take a joke about
but I didn't want another one
knowing that as soon as we got more than
nine boys in our two grades in our room
I could be bat boy
or mere spectator
standing with relief
and the girls
watching the clouds

(when I wasn't praying for rain
 I was talking seriously to god
 about immigrants)

those days are with me yet
or else I would not be writing this poem
having come inside from a too warm day

---

heavy with possible rain
that stirred in me a fear
that at first I could not figure out
until my township school days came
suddenly over me with their overalls
and work shoes with holes in the toes
and I almost cried twice:
once for present relief
and once for my small self
out there in right field

praying so goddamned hard
for that rain that never came

MARJORIE MAIN

I am marjorie main
ma kettling her kids
to come and get it
with a fervor
matched only by
my grandfather
railing at republicans

there is so much of me growing up
in seeing ma kettle and her rocking chair husband
yell their way through yet another movie
while I giggled and hid my face in guffaws
and jujy fruits

that is me growing up
because my grandmother was marjorie main
or at least a damned good look alike
with her white hair
her square jaw set to yell at people
in the next room
or because she was a bit deaf
right in your ear as you bent over
the potato salad once again

she looked like the mountain people
that old lady main represented
her lack of good teeth setting her mouth
in from the rest of her face
her white hair in wisps around her ears
her stance not quite genteel
but more hard and necessary and rural
as she yelled at grandpa to come in from
the barn to eat noontime dinner

she puttered in her ma kettle kitchen
setting out dishes of things to eat
that would drive a gourmet wild:

kool aid without sugar because it was forgot
ham fried and salted until it curled
in desperate but useless self defense
the silverware kept in a glass in the middle
of the heavy wooden table
and newspapers spread over everything
after every meal to keep the flies from
getting what was left

my uncles in from the fields
slurped their coffee
with my grandfather
pouring it too hot from
saucer to cup and back again
while I stared at
this the second of wonders
surpassed only by my mother's father
calmly eating peas on a knife
and I not able to get my own
in a spoon from the cracked plate
to my mouth

it was forbidden to interrupt my grandfather
at twelve sharp when he listened to the hog report
and the other farmer news on the cincinnati station
chicago's decisions to pay us so much per pound
for our pork and chickens and our bushels of grain
ripped from the fields surrounding the house
added to all the other fields worth across the land
that became what was talked of around the world

marjorie main is dead
but a few days
my grandmother a few years more
but the memory of them both
causing me to laugh
at their delightful interpretations
of life brings no real sadness now

but a bit of reflective love
as I remember the nights at the hines theater
while picking out the jujy fruits from my molars
as I remember the days with my grandma
slipping sugar into the kool aid
and how I loved them both

the only tragic figures
in the whole plot
are those poor pieces of ham
curling and cringing in the skillet
sizzling their lives away
on a wood burning stove
somewhere in a different age
in indiana

BLACKBERRY WINTER

blackberry winter my wife calls it
when june turns cold after hot may
and sweaters are unfolded
when not already mothballed
and coffee cups are held in two hands
as we purr in the chilled sunlight
fighting its way
through the window glass
to get inside to its own warmth

blackberry winter she calls it
and I remember picking berries
and seeing my pigment change
finding relief in standing up
and rubbing the small of my back
and arching my usual stooped shoulders
backwards wanting it all somehow
to snap and pop into place
but instead bending over once again
to reach for the stainers of my fingers
privately throwing some now and then
into my mouth
and later grinning away my secret
by showing my two tone teeth

blackberry winter:
a nice name for a respite
before the sidewalks
fry eggs for front pages
and the intensity of the weather
again becomes the first thing
one mentions when one walks
through dark wooden screen doors
marked wonder bread and welcome
greeted by sure hot ain't it
and you say sure is
before you dare ask for

whatever you want to carry back
into that heat that reminds you
not of other hot times
but of your wife smiling at you
across the ray of sunshine
holding her coffee cup
in her strong brown hands
telling you of the
blackberry winters of her youth

WES AND NORY

write
write
just start writing this poem
and see if it gets anywhere
or see if maybe you just have
to quit and say
to hell with it
and go to bed after all

remember how you used to prime the gray pump
down the road at wes and nory's place
after they had died
and the sheep were
being kept there
remember how you had to pour the water
into the top of the pump
so it could give up its gasping
and start giving water back

and the day you went down and found the sheep
eaten by the dogs
torn apart and still alive some of them
and others bloating in the sun already
and dad had to shoot the ones
with entrails on view
and you had to prime the pump just the same
if not more so
to give those that did not die
the liquid in their wooden trough

remember priming the pump
cause it's the same technique here
to run the words across the paper
and see if they and others jump back at you

sometimes it works and sometimes it doesn't
and sometimes I'm just not sure

but I am sure about those sheep
rotting in the hot afternoon
and the enormous blue flies
buzzing and buzzing
giving a horrid noise to the scene
spread out before us on the lot
where those who had got away
stood baahing for their water
while I got the pump readied
and tried not to see what
was over the fence
wishing my nose had such a choice

before the sheep
before I ever primed that pump
wes and nory were alive
and sitting on their swing
that faced our house
going back and forth
before wes died and nory moved into town
as farm widows do
before she sat in her small town house
before she was suddenly
laid in a coffin
shriveled and tiny
for me to cry over after school
while two women
in the back of the parlor
guessed and stagewhispered
that I must be the town paper boy
and I resented their intrusion
into our lives
as nory and I remembered
my thousands of daily barefoot visits
to her porch swing
and her cookies
and her chatter about nothing important
and everything important
and how I used to tease her
about her brick sidewalk

all fifteen feet of it
from that porch to the metal gate
that led to the mailbox
where arizona highways sat glistening orange
every month or so

her brick sidewalk all two bricks wide
that she lifted up each late spring
and cleaned out between each brick
so that it was fresh and dark red
and ready for summer feet such as mine
that would bring news of no importance
and all importance
from our house one full quarter mile down the road
sitting on our hill
looking at that little house of hers
where she and wes
went on living
in the living room that smelled
of stuffed horsehair and oiled furniture
of a radio always on
and wallpaper never changed
a living room that led agreeably
to the porch swing

where I scraped my feet
on the boards of the porch itself
as I maneuvered it back and forth
flaking the rust off the chain
that I jerked back and forth
as much I dared

something I now joke about
is the trip we six took to new england
when I gave up that porch swing
for two whole weeks:
I vowed great gifts to wes and wife
and she said only a handkerchief
would do quite nice
and nothing more than that

but I in my generous way with
all my eight dollars
saved from now god knows what
said no
and fourteen days later
brought her a handkerchief
which she took in both hands
as if it were the holy grail
and I slipped wes his
partially eaten maple sugar
candy from vermont
that barely made it back
in the glove compartment
through all those states
and all those afternoons

strangers to me now live in that house
and I wonder if the brick sidewalk survived
but I dare not stop
for I fear an answer either way

so I pass the house no longer green
no swing on the porch
no pump in the yard
the sidewalk
perhaps gone
perhaps buried
perhaps kept just so just yet

the pasture near the house remains
awaiting more sheep
more dogs
more boys with screams caught in their throats

priming
priming
priming

TWINE

my father fixed the farm with twine
that pulled and rotted black
and died its annual death

and so to bring renewal
the two of us
would walk
hauling new string
together round the farm

as I bit my lip
then let go
against the fury of it all
and cried aloud
that fences fixed with twine
did not last
and looked homemade at that
but my father smiled
and continued to macrame his life into
the rusty breaking fences
of the eighty acre farm
he still calls home

I was never more ashamed than when
he fixed those fences with baler twine
I wanted bright red metal fences
around the fields
to tell everyone that
the barn that needed painting
the house that needed painting
were but eccentricities
and not a measure of our true worth

but in farm country
everyone knows that everyone knows
and there would have been no use
in trying to disguise our too well known state

so we continued to tie the twine
and pull together the rusty metal pieces
of fences put up a generation or two before
when men went out to the fields with
posts of new wood
and rolls of town bought metal fencing
and hope that that year
the crop would come through
that would release them
from the land they so hated and so loved
lacking visions of later men tied to the farm
lives of twine rotting black in the sun
that neighbors clucked tongues over
as they drove by and spotted the white and black
fences being made by a smiling father
and a raging son standing by a ball of twine
somewhere far too short of plenty

KETCHUP

I never liked my mother's ketchup
but all the other homemade things
that surfaced in the kitchen
were admired
finger tested
and then wolfed down
as smiling universal proof
that what had only recently been there
had been briefly but furiously appreciated

but my mother's ketchup
was too strong and didn't have
the gentle flavor of what
I had learned to like in
formica tabled truck stops
and how ya doin restaurants of
our visits to town
her ketchup was a flop
and she must have realized it herself
for it took only a few years
for her to stop making it
and giving it to us
at the table

(I preferred the fruit pies
bubbling in their glass plates
sitting as proud of themselves
as she was of them
on the top of the range
enticing that young boy
who could not
who simply could not
keep his finger from touching
a bit of the crust
and a bit of the bubble
even those meant for sunday school picnics
and saturday night ice cream socials

burning his finger
and getting admonished
by someone who was proud of
the irresistibility of the child
yet who wanted desperately to
take a whole pie
somewhere sometime)

I never liked my mother's ketchup
the smell in the kitchen was enough
and perhaps because she had too many whole bottles

testifying on the cellar shelf
she decided years later to put that chore aside
and stick with pies

TILE

I used to lay tile
cutting my hands on the orange
round pieces that disappeared
into the ground to later
hold the water on its way from
the sky to the creek

I used to lay tile
an easy job
and one which farmers did
when all those other things were done
an important job if one were not content
with standing water in the fields
after a hard rain
drowning the corn or leaving it
too yellow at
the end of the row
by the fence that needed repairing
the farmer hoping it was hidden from
the critical eyes of the neighbors
who gossiped loudly shouting at each other
over tractor noises about so and so's corn
and how it looked bad

it was inexcusable to have a crooked row
of corn or soybeans
or to have thistles in your wheat
or not to help the neighbor lay his tile
when he had helped you with yours

I used to lay tile
standing in for my father
who worked in town
and who pushed pencils along the paper
as I put the tile down into the trench
or more likely handed them to others
to lay so gently down

just so far apart
to let the water in
but not the soil

laying tile satisfied the anal in us
so good it was to tile a field
so that the next rain would be foiled
and the crops would prosper
not too wet
not too dry
but just right for the later harvest
we set the tile deep enough
to avoid the plow
but high enough to do some good

the mounds of rows of dirt
after we were done
lay there as witness to our day long deeds
then silently disappeared in the weeks to come
until the field was again grass covered
and dry

I used to lay tile
scarring my hands
afraid to wear gloves and be the only one
rubbing them together at the end of the afternoon
as we surveyed a finished field
and noted how we had beaten the elements once again
how the field would look
when the gray clouds became quickly white
and all the corn next year turned green
and fit for a neighbor's remark
and a good sale at the mill

SPOON

it was the sort of restaurant where they made
you keep your spoon
was the first line I carried around
in a pocket in my mind for so many months
dreaming of the quiet evening I would sit down
at this typewriter and whack out a great poem
where the second and third lines
would lead me further into something joyous

instead I tried
but came up with some banal words
that are going into the waste basket
as soon as this piece of paper
makes its way out of the machine

some disappointment
a lot of shoulder shrugging
and I told you sos said to myself
adding: I should not savor lines quite so much
as they grow stale
dry up
crack
rot
wither
become impotent
once I finally sit down
smugly assuming a poem will follow

I even told my wife
I was carrying around this line
waiting until I was ready
to put it on paper
and follow it up with gobs more

as it is:
I got this poem about poems
but there is not the satisfaction

I might have had had I written
something stupendous about restaurants I have known
with green vinyl booths
metal rimmed formica tops
long flat black grills
where envied men stood scraping hamburger grease
off into mysterious wells at the back side

and waitresses stared in disbelief at
my inconsiderate behavior at leaving my
spoon on my first course plate
and who said to me in a tired voice
accustomed to saying such things:
keep your spoon

MEMORIES

I am waiting for my daughter's first memory

.last night as I put her to bed
and kissed the side of her face
her grin letting me know that was pure ecstasy
though she insisted loudly that she was not
wanting kisses but privacy
I wondered if she would remember anything
of that day to carry into the future
and decided instantly that she would not
probably nor will I
unless I get here
a poem worth keeping

my first memory is running into the rusty metal fence
that then ran up and down our lane
hurting my butt by crashing against it
and having to take down my pants
and show the scars to my parents
assuring them through my tears
that all of me was indeed going to live

or else it was swinging in the orchard
pumping as fast as I could
shouting the swing back and forth
the old board resigned to one more
frantic afternoon
standing there stark naked
as surprised drivers went by
honking to warn my mother
that a preschool kid
was playing havoc with his body
and she rescued me
with a smack on that very behind
she had so carefully wanted preserved
only one stanza away

or maybe it was arriving in north carolina
seated in my little wooden chair
that I had sat in all the way from home
so that I wouldn't miss anything
having my uncle in his voice
we could not understand
say hello
coughing
between cigarettes
and opening the door for my mother
so she could take his wife into her arms

I wonder what my daughter will remember
what will be the first thing
to spring into her consciousness
when people years and years later
say to one another sitting on couches
or pillows on the floor:
what's the first thing you remember

I would like to think
it would be replied to
by the following:
my father leaning over to kiss me good night
before he went downstairs to write another poem

I like to think that
even though it may not prove true
she may not remember me kissing her last night
though her present memory serves well enough
to remind her that every night I take her into my arms
and sigh filled with thoughts much too deep

I do not intend for her to get too big
for her dad to lean over
and kiss her goodnight
that I will not allow
only to belong now to me and a little girl
lying in bed

eyes closed
face in a suppressed giggle
as I bend over
as is my habit
and put one more kiss
into her
memories

BOOTS

I simply cannot wear boots
even those shiny leather zippered ones
so in fashion with so many
I simply cannot wear boots
having worn work shoes
to grade school
year after year
rough brown shoes
that always needed orange oil
to soak into the skin
to make it smooth and breathing
looking back I can't remember
wearing those shoes
more than three or four years
but the weight of how they looked
when I went into town
pulls yet at my feet
and forbids them to step into
merely modern versions
of the same thing

it signaled me a farmer
something I did not at that time
in my life want to own up to being

I was caught in the middle of things
my father not qualifying as a full time farmer
with my peers
his working in town and hustling
the tractor around
at night
not enough for him to be an
honest to goodness
haymow and feedlot fellow
and at the same time
our living on eighty acres
six miles from town

with rusting machinery sitting in a barnyard
and manure wafting its way to your nostrils
was enough in the eyes and noses
of the town folk to say we were
farmers enough

the last pair of farmer shoes I owned
were worn in my eighth school year
worn so much that I got a hole in the toe
of one of the pair
making them only look worse
with a lack of a sense of fashion
it took me half a year
to realize that the other boys in my class
no longer wore those shoes
but had traded them off at least while in school
for low cut ones
black and brown
with soft laces and
a decidedly grown up look

I asked for the same thing
and got my wish
saying something to my mother
in the kitchen at christmas time
and went back to school
the next month
in my own version of
non farm shoes
and have not worn any since

in seventh grade
I tried to be cute and trip
another kid and
instead landed on my right hand
on the cement floor
and wore a cast on that arm
for six long weeks
being examined in the hospital

that first painful day
I was mortified to know that
my shoes stuck up in the air
for the nurses to see
knowing full well that a very small
piece of manure rested in that place
between the heel and the sole
that place that one usually scraped
off against those flat black
upright pieces of metal
posted outside doors of clean homes

but this time I had forgotten
and remembered only
when I lay on the table
my arm throbbing beside me
the smell of manure
I was sure filling the room
making people faint outside the door

if the truth be known
I doubt they noticed at all

my sister beth
wanted me to stop coming in
to the drugstore where she worked
because I bothered her while she
was trying to work
because I tried to con her out of
a pepsi and nabs and usually won
because I wore in her words:
those shoes
footwear she found offensive
and reminders of where we all came from

she was town
desperately town
and I was too young to appreciate
that I should have faded into the five and ten

and buried my head in comics
or browsed the hardware store
instead of clumping into her domain
with my heavy dark farm shoes
and my look of the rural unwashed

I must have found those shoes somewhat traumatic
and I don't know now why I wore them
so long so patiently
maybe I did try to get others but could not
as it seemed senseless to have one pair of shoes
to wear to school and another to do the chores in
and besides if the other boys were wearing them
then I must wear them too

but I still say:
I must have found those shoes somewhat traumatic
if today I cannot look at a pair of men's boots
or any shoes that make their way above the ankle
without thinking to myself:
I simply cannot wear boots
and I run ankles exposed to my own closet
where my pairs of low cut shoes rest
waiting to have their shoe trees torn from them
and my feet thrust in them
to go dancing through the day

and I look at them with relief
knowing my feet will not betray me
that I will not be pointed out on the street
wearing a pair of old brown high top shoes
reeking of orange oil and manure
giving the pointer the excuse to say
to his companion:

farmer

my peculiar ethnic epithet
that angers me more now than it did

when actually uttered
because now I realize
epithets are like boomerangs
said in terms of:

amish
jew

a farmer born and now farm proud

but instead I blend with the town people
each with his own hangups
they not guessing that mine is
the absolute necessity of wearing low cut shoes
thinking somehow that if I were to wear a
pair of boots
I would reek oil and manure
and be thrown off the bus

but instead I put my feet inside low cut shoes
shoes I put on the tops of tables
when I want to lean back and relax
shoes I put there with some modicum of pride
let alone a knowledge that no small piece of manure
rests on the underside for all to see
nor does oil reek the room

shoes a sister could be proud of

BEMBERG OR NYLON

bemberg or nylon
she used to ask
and we all laughed
and voted
on which so called good dress
she should wear
away from the place
where her small number
of housedresses
repaired and ironed
waited
to be retrieved
once their better counterpart
had returned to its hanger

now:
my mother has more than two dresses
her suitcase is full
of her things
on infrequent visits
and the phrase
we tease is one
that recalls
where we've been
and where we are now:

bemberg or nylon

the bitterness that could not then surface
for fear it would release much more
is no longer necessary
as two weeks worth of clothes
for three days of staying
is carted upstairs
and outfits appear
new ones each meal
still homemade

(we aren't that far away
 from those years)
but flaunted
like bemberg and nylon never were

in a world where women
had only two dresses
there was no problem
with such a choice
but in town with windows
full of mannequins mocking
the farm women
trudging by with rough flat hands
and dresses made of feedsacks
there was a need to
rub too quickly together
the two palms
and worry quick hard worries
about more clothes
had not one other things
like new jeans for late august
and money for farm notes
and trying to meet at least partially
the dreams of girls
entering ninth grade
into a world of those from town
who had more than one sweater
and no chores to do after school

our worry about rain
was quite enough to bind us
and separate us from
those in town
who worried only about parades
and lawns where hoses
came out during those weeks
we stood with our hands to our foreheads
brows furrowed like spring fields
and looked to heaven for water

or on other days dark with drizzle
wanted moisture more evenly spread

women who remained
as widows on farms
run by sons or neighbors sons
shook their heads
at the dim noon light and
laughed quietly sometimes
at town peoples ways
teased perhaps by those same more
comfortable sons with a quick phrase:

bemberg or nylon

bringing quiet chuckles
and seemingly absent minded
nods of the head
while pausing over noodles
in a kitchen
away from the
unsuspecting town

CRUSTS

only two womens crusts will I eat
particular about my pies
and my women
I hold that only two can do
what makes my stomach
leap in anticipation
and later in thankful humility
when the crust is resting
chunks and chunks of it
soaked in the particular
filling resting in my stomach
before that part of my body
attacks what my mouth
has so furiously and quickly
already gotten to

rhubarb is the best
though seconds could be many:
hot raisin glazed
cherry or strawberry
apple in a variety of ways

where the two women differ in pies
is where they differ
in their backgrounds:

my wife serving me for the first time
sweet potato pie swore that it
was not my mother's pumpkin
and only the ingredients' remains
waiting on the sink counter
served to convince me that
I was on to something new
that tasted old

the first rhubarb
she made was with
a bit of trepidation
but my lowering myself
to my knees
and kissing hers
and saying only half
mocking to one already betrothed
marry me and I'll take care of you
forever as long as you keep making
rhubarb pie proved to her that
she had once again met my needs

other pies can't come up to snuff
as my mother used to say
hard dark crusts
dry particles fit to choke a horse
pieces of baked dough
not ready for anyone's palate
but good perhaps for door stops
on windy days or
flooring in an old barn
or something given to someone
you no longer like

only two womens crusts will I eat
and those two women know it
smiling smugly at each other
in the kitchen
wiping their hands
on terry cloth towels
watching me wolf down yet another piece
not allowed to cool lest someone else
discover the treasure and deprive me
of my anointed wedges
women who do not compete for
the honor of my pausing to exhale

smile and dive in once again
but who know simply that I
say to them both:

only two womens crusts will I eat

I WANT TO WRITE POEMS

I want to write poems
about the way the wood
siding on old buildings
on the farm I grew up on
starts to pull away from
those buildings at the bottom
and how it turns black
and then green with moss
each board standing a little off
the others so that they make
a kind of pattern that would
not be unlike a series of
slightly curved and independent
pieces of something
leaning into the wall

I want to write about how
the grass grows up between
those boards at the bottom
and how the vines grow snakelike
between them pushing them further
apart from each other and how
those vines then go inside
the building in a snoopy sort
of way looking for light so they
can go straight up or almost so
and out some crack at the top
buildings like that have cracks
at the top where shingles have long
since blown off and have not been
replaced or put back with nails
that won't allow rust streaks
to go down the sides of the
building

I beg to mention the rose bushes
that sometimes are found along

buildings like that
shielding the vines from the
lawn mower
that comes along frustrated
in its attempt to get at that
grass that is between the curved
out boards

the bushes with their
damned thorns stand guard
over the building
that is much worse off than one
might imagine looking only at
the roses crowded together in
the early summer holding up their
dozens of pale pink faces to you as if
they were bare shoulders on a not
terribly shy young woman's body that
is clothed in a gown that reveals
her rounded figure

might I also talk about the
cracked bit of old sidewalk
that runs up against one end of that
building so many cracks filled with
grass and with dirt that is pushing
the pieces to be so uneven
somewhere might be scratched a date
when a father and son most likely
poured the cement onto the ready
ground when that building was young
and the boards stood straight
against the inside wood and the
paint on the building was not so
awfully gone and the son watches
his son or grandson nowadays
walk barefoot over the cracks
and tries to remember what else was
happening that summer when he and

his dad poured the white thick
lumpy stuff onto the ground to make
the first sidewalk this farm had
ever known

let me bring this to a close by
mentioning that man walking determinedly
so as not to appear quite so old as he
feels over those cracks wanting that
building to look as it did when he was
a small boy as he sees in the buildings
demise his own
the building has an excuse:
it's been outside for seventy years
the paint was not often enough replaced
the winters were sometimes bad
with snow piled against it for weeks

he and the building are friends
as trees like creeks
and neighbors houses outlined against
the horizon like the sky they
snuggle against
as the sun is going down
the man goes in shoes over the cracks
remembering every so many months
that there was a date marked in
that sidewalk once but it was on the
end where the cement was shallower and
it split off before his son was born
he reckons the date
vows to cut out the vines
promises to fix the boards
back against the building
and wonders if the pain would be
worth the time and trouble

DRINKING CUP

write a poem sometime he said
about the rusty drinking cup
we used to drink out of
at the well in front of her house

he had commented on how much
he liked the poem about our
mutual grandmother
and her marjorie main ways

and he was gently reminding me
of the other thing I had failed
to mention

I could taste that cup
when he said it
and I nodded at the phone
and made a note to speak of it
in a poem someday

now four years later
I am here to tell you
about a cup that tasted of rust
and water that was country deep
and smacked of iron

I am tasting it now
and I can barely write this poem
for licking my lips
and swallowing well water
once again

THE PRETTIEST

the prettiest stood at the front:
she was the preacher
the next to the prettiest stood to the side:
she sang bringing in the sheaves
the next to the next to the prettiest sobbed:
the official mourner
while the baby rabbit
was put to rest
under three inches of topsoil
and a bouquet of weeds

the prettiest was put to rest
with a room full of storebought flowers
while the next to and the next to the next to
leaned their bodies against one another
and stared into the coffin
not quite fifty years later

all of us wondering:
where did it all go

CRAYONS

I hated the children with 48 crayons

theatre seats of colors
belonging to fortunate kids

my sixteen separated me
from the eight of
the truly poor

but even my reasonable box
reminded me of
a tired woman
pulling nickels from her light weight purse
buying new overalls
sewing shirts
taking crayons off the shelf
pushing aside the 48
as unreal as visiting dress shops
instead of bolts of fabric on sale

I like to think my life
has been brilliantly cast in sixteen colors
and in thousands of hues

while those children
drowned in their father's green
describe a sunset as red

I now hold my crayons high in the air
far from the grasping too late
hands of the children
who would not share their
other thirty two
with me

BACK HOME

back home:
do the dogs
still get in the sheep
spilling entrails like fun
across the too short grass

do high school girls
still stare out kitchen windows
waiting for their moms
to come home from town
so they can tell them
they'll be grandmothers
by christmas for sure

back home:
do they still bell newlyweds
and have open caskets at funeral parlors
and gossip on the sidewalks in front of churches
about the drunks
and the too easy even in easier times

I hope that of all that may still be
that the dogs do not get in the sheep
that they do nothing to
horrify school boys
coming suddenly upon scenes of war

but I know that as surely as
presidents still send soldiers to kill and be killed
dogs carry out their own horrid primeval urges

and woolen bodies lie across the
fields of their own
flanders and shilohs

back home

TELL THEM THIS WHEN I DIE

oh I went barefoot quite enough
drank well water
tore my skin against corn leaves
ducked from the flying blood
of a chicken suddenly headless
held brother sheep while their nuts
were removed

and I grasped for mine

COTTONWOOD — *in progress*

first it was the cottonwood

gone she said on the phone
cut down while we watched

the bedroom picture window
for once showed too much of the world
and they had to turn away
while the old tree along the ditch
fell over onto the land they no longer owned

why couldn't he have waited
we all said
waited until they left
just another few years
how many ears of corn could he add
with the loss of that old tree

every year the white gentle puffs
came blowing into my face
and I laughed and brushed them away
the cottonwood is out
I would cry
not really having to tell anyone
who was outside at the back of the house

they blew onto
the smokehouse
the woodhouse
the pig houses
the grainary
the old garage almost too narrow for modern cars

all those buildings now gone too
remaining are the house and barn
the civil war adze marks harshly cut into the beams
the old cellar where I just knew escaping slaves had hid

and was angry that I could find no proof
all I asked for was one spoon
or a note somehow kept dry for one century

for most of this century my father lived in the house
his only home
the room in which he will sleep for three more weeks
the same room where he was born after sarajevo and before the
luisitania

my mother came as a teenager
a bride from mere fields away

now like the cottonwood
they will leave
blown north to the retirement home
where lives are compressed into fewer rooms
pictures on the small fridge
frozen into third grades or graduation gowns
somehow meant to capture generations

I think I know every tree
every turn of the creek
every strip of wallpaper
and piece of woodwork

when the porches were still both open to the wind
when we listened to big radio in the living room
when the winter stove was the warming place for our clothes

the kitchen table was where we gathered
filling out record books for the county fair
writing thank you letters to aunts in cities
addressing penny valentines to everyone in the class
as we were one of those children who gave everyone one
whether we liked them or not

a mother's rule became our own when we had our own

my parents have sprinkled valentines around the county

all their lives from the farmhouse they will now leave
behind

no more will I pull over the hill from the west
and see the house splashed white against the sun
smelling already the chicken and noodles
and seeing hands wiping supper onto aprons
and grease and oil onto work pants

home is where the heart is
and our heart is there
but mostly with them
so when they go
our heart will go too

yet we leave a bigger piece than we can imagine
back there with the room where we used to call out
that we were thirsty and our father came to our door
unfailingly with a glass and a yawn
back there with the door
where my father outtalked the witnesses of jehovah
the room where my mother with pins in her mouth
made our clothes that we could not afford in stores

and we leave a piece of ourselves on the bank of the creek
where ploughs and disks have already covered over
the rough hole where the cottonwood stood
during my fathers boyhood and mine

when my parents head slowly down the drive
crunching the gravel
stopping surely on the road to take a last look
there shall be a rough hole
where all of us have been ripped out
leaving behind the farm
without the cottonwood

without us

About the Author

John Sherman returned to live in his native Indiana in 1985, after nearly 20 years in Nigeria, Ghana, Malawi, Zaire, Washington, D.C., and Santa Fe. Raised on a farm in the northeastern part of the state, he now lives in Indianapolis where he owns a public relations firm.

This is Sherman's third book of poetry. His poems have appeared in dozens of little and literary magazines and in poetry anthologies. His poetry has earned him first-place and best-of-issue honors from magazines and sponsoring organizations. He has given numerous readings of his poetry and short fiction in Washington, D.C., Santa Fe, and Indianapolis. In Santa Fe, he participated in a two-man reading with the noted poet Gerald Stern. Sherman lectured and read poetry at Miami-Dade Community College in a program funded in part by the Florida Endowment for the Humanities. He also served as Poet in Residence at Brevard Community College in Florida.

He also writes fiction and nonfiction. Some of his stories have appeared in various literary magazines around the country. His feature writing and photography have been widely published in major newspapers and magazines. For several years, he wrote a weekly humor column, "Generally Sherman," for the *Santa Fe Reporter*. His book, *Santa Fe: A Pictorial History,* earned him the New Mexico Governor's Award for Historic Preservation. He later wrote a companion volume, *Taos: A Pictorial History.*

A member of the Authors' Guild and the Writers' Center of Indianapolis, Sherman is listed in *A Directory of American Poets and Fiction Writers.*

Photo Credits

Front cover:
Photo of Mary Etta and John Scholer taken in the kitchen of the author's parents, John F. and Dorothy Sherman, 1961 (photo by John F. Sherman).

Dedication:
Wedding photo of Mary Etta and John Scholer, December 26, 1899 (J.H. Schwartz Studio, Portland, Indiana). Dale Scholer, eighth-grade graduation photo, School No. 4, Noble Township, Jay County, Indiana, 1922 (photographer unknown).

This page:
Left to right, Rosalind (next-to-the-prettiest), Beth (next-to-the-next-to-the-prettiest), and Janice (the prettiest), author's sisters, 1942 (photo by John F. Sherman).

Back Cover:
Photo of author, circa 1953 (photo by John F. Sherman).